CHILDREN T... E SUN

by
George Wells
Parker

Editor's Note:

The Children of the Sun was first published in 1918 by the Hamitic League of the World. Black Classic Press reprinted it first in 1978, and again in 1981. Our press was founded with the intention of bringing to light obscure and significant works by and about people of African descent.

With the republication of Mr. Parker's classic work we hope to end the obscurity that surrounds him and Children of the Sun. It is also our hope that the republication of this work will cause it's significance to be shared by a larger interested body of people, especially those for whom Mr. Parker originally wrote this work — The Children of the Sun.

W. Paul Coates
September 2, 1981

ISBN-13 978-0-933121-10-2
ISBN-10 0-933121-10-5

First published 1918 by the Hamitic League of the World, republished 1978, 1981 Black Classic Press

AFRICA

Behold!
The Sphinx is Africa. The bond
Of silence is upon her.
Old
And white with tombs, and rent and shorn;
With raiment wet with tears and torn,
And trampled on, yet all untamed;
All naked now, yet not ashamed,—
The mistress of the young world's prime,
Whose obelisk's still laugh at Time,
And lift to heaven her fair name,
Sleeps satisfied upon her fame.
Who shall say:
My father reared a pyramid;
My brother clipped the dragon's wings;
My mother was Semirimis?
Yea, harps strike idly out of place;
Men sing of savage Saxon kings
New-born and known but yesterday.
—"The Ship In the Desert," Joaquin Miller.

THE CHILDREN OF THE SUN

In the morning of the world, when the fingers of Love swept aside the curtains of Time, our dusky mother, Ethiopia, held the stage. It was she who wooed civilization and gave birth to nations. Egypt was her first-born and to Ur of the Chaldees she sent her sons and daughters, who scattered empires in Asia as the wanton winds of autumn scatter the seeds of flowers. Beside the beautiful Mediterranean she build'ed Phoenicia, and in ships with purple sails she sent her children to the blue Aegean, there to found Greece, the marvel of men and the queen of history. Troy was hers, and from that burning city fled swarthy Aeneas, who set the ferment for Rome, the Eternal City. Her spirit called to Arabia and out of the mystic deserts surged the black soldiers of Islam, who welded the world into a new empire and sang their songs of love and victory in the vales of Andalusia. On the isles of all the oceans, and from where the Southern Cross bends low to kiss the restless waves to where the Arctic holds in leash its frozen world, her hand has touched. Religion, art, literature, science and civilization are hers, and eternity but lives in the warmth of her radiant glow. I have chosen to call the unnumbered millions of her descendants the Children of the Sun.

AFRICA

A little more than a century ago a Frenchman by the name of Volney wrote an eloquent book entitled, "Ruins of Empires." It so delighted the scholars of the day that it was translated into English and a special edition sent across the Atlantic, to be known as the American edition. The translator, out of respect to the feelings of Americans respecting the black races, left out the following quotation: "There are a people, now forgotten, discovered, while others were yet barbarians, the elements of the arts and sciences. A race of men ejected from society for their sable skin and frizzled hair founded, on the study of the laws of Nature, those civil and religious systems which still govern the universe." Years after, when Volney mastered the English language and discovered how the truth had been surrendered to prejudice, he requested that all future editions contain the suppressed words or else the entire work be taken out of print.

This incident, which so clearly manifests the attitude of the early Americans toward the truth concerning the black race, has scarcely changed with passing years. Today there is not a single book printed in the English language that tells the wonderful work of the archeologists in Africa, Asia, and Europe, and how this work has vindicated the African race as the real founder of human civilization. During the year of 1873 Herr Reinisch, a Viennese Egyptologist, startled the scholars of Europe by saying that not only were the Egyptians of African origin, but that "the human races of the ancient world, of Europe and Africa, are descended from a single family, whose original seat was on the shores of Equatorial Africa." At that time the science of human races was in its infancy and its students were not prepared for so sweeping an assertion. All kinds of wild speculations and ridiculous theories were rife, and it was expected that this doctrine of Reinisch would pass with the vagaries of the day. Yet now, after thirty-five years, the University of Pennsylvania reports a remarkably succesful archeological expedition which, it says, will completely overthrow the long established standards, not only of history but of ethnology as well. The university assures us that Negro art is primarily original and that civilization probably had its rise in the great lake regions of the African continent.

Africa is the enigma of all continents. It is still the land of mystery and many surprises yet await the adventurer who travels her long lost paths in search of knowledge. Scholars have already found problems that have outwitted them. Frobenius, a well known scientist, has voiced this clearly when he says: "We ethnologists have fared particularly ill. Far from bringing answers to our questions, the travlers have increased our enigma by many an addition so peculiar that astonishment has scarce yet made room for investigation. For the pictures of the inhabitants and the specimens of their civilization are indeed, questions. Open an illustrated geography and compare the 'type of African Negro,' the bluish-black fellow of the protuberant lips, the flattened nose, the stupid expression, the short, curly hair, with the tall, bronze figures from Dark Africa, with which we have of late come in contact, their almost fine-cut features, long hair, etc., you have an example pressing for solution."

The excavation carried on under the supervision of the Pennsylvania University are located in the regions of lower Nubia and in the neighborhoood of the ancient seat of the great Empire of Ethiopia. Tradition has it that Ethiopia is the mother of nations and that she nourished and reared not only Egypt, but many of the nations of Asia and even gave to Greece her gods, laws and civilization. In spite of the fact that Ridpath (whose publishers admit that he is a popular historian and not an acurrate one) classifies the Ethiopians as white, it seems that their very name is Greek for "the duskyfaced ones," and the phrase,"to wash the Ethiopian white," was a proverbial expression applied by the ancients to a hopeless task. The Hebraical verse, "Can the Ethiopian change his skin or the leopard his spots?" is yet another verification of the fact that the Ethiopians of six thousand years ago were the same as the Ethiopians of today. Greece seems to have had a respect for the Ethiopians that amounted to almost reverence. To them Ethiopia was the home of a divine people, and from Ethiopia came their great god Zeus. Of them Homer sings:

> "The sire of gods and all the ethereal train,
> On the warm limits of the farthest main,
> Now mix with mortals, nor disdain to grace
> The feasts of Ethiopia's blameless race."——(Illiad.)

It has been written that "when the Greeks knew scarcely of Italy or Sicily by name, the virtues, the civilization and the mythology of the Ethiopian supplied their poets a subject of lofty description." Diodorus tells us that they were the inventors of pomps, sacrifices, solemn assemblies and of all honors paid the gods. Herodotus accounted them as a wonderful race and the Hebrews paid them lofty tribute in their scriptures. A very close relationship existed between the Egyptians and the Ethiopians. It is nowhere asserted that both spoke the same language, but this seems implied and very probable in view of the fact that their hieroglyphics are the same. In religion their relationship was even more pronounced. Both had the same system of worship, the same sacredotal orders, the same pomps and processions. The images of the gods were at certain times conveyed up the Nile from their Egyptian temples to others in Ethiopia and after the festival were brought back again into Egypt. Many times in the history of Egypt the country swayed under Ethiopian dynasties.

There are other things that make Ethiopia great even to this day. Her country is one of the few that has never bowed down to a conqueror and her government is the oldest known to human history, China not excepted. In the Kebro Negest, the official record of the royal family, appear the names of her kings in unbroken succession from the time of Solomon till the present day, and only fancy can dream how far back into the shadowy ages this line of black monarchs ruled. If it be true that governments are instituted among men for the promotion of happiness and well being, then this empire is one of the few nations of the world that has approached near to the realization of this ideal. Her system of government is communal. In all her history no hereditary nobility was ever known; no caste of priests ever existed. Between ruler and people there can and could be nothing, and every one might aspire equally to all the honors of state or to the highest dignity of the priesthood. Let it be said for them, and said truly, that they first conceived the true principles of the universal human liberty and founded the first government upon the eternal truth that all governments should derive their just powers from the consent of the governed. From the dawn of their history until today woman has always been the equal of man, and in no country until the present did pictures of domestic felicity play so large a part as they did in ancient Ethiopia.

"What is history," once asked the great Napoleon, "but a fiction agreed upon?" How truly has this agreement been kept by all American historians whenever the black races have been concerned! With what pains have they undertaken to say that certain peoples of antiquity were "not Negroes" and that "Negroes appear upon the monuments of ancients as slaves only."

What standing can such historians as Ridpath and Myers and others have with scholars when they classify the Ethiopian as a branch of the Caucasian race? Could the weeping Jeremiah but know that with a drop of ink an American has proven his logic faulty, he might then believe that a leopard can change its spots and that those accustomed to do evil are capable of good. There is absolutely no grounds for such erroneous statements in the light of modern science. They may call Herodotus the father of lies instead of the father of history; they may say that the author of Genesis had a weakness for genealogy and decided to settle the vexed questions of racial origins by writing faulty ancestral records; possible, too, that all other scribes and travelers suffered from diseases of mind and memory; but the tangible records in stone which these departed of earth's guests left behind them in token of their existence cannot be false. Whatever science has done or may do, one thing is certain: it has with indisputable evidence, in stone and picture, established for all time that the African was the master and not the slave, the conqueror and not the conquered, the civilized and not the savage.

When our minds wander back to the mystic maze of human beginnings they linger longest over that mysterious land through which flows the sacred Nile. Whence came the first people who trod its alluvial plain? Were they Nigritic wanderes from Equatorial Africa or Semites from lands beyond the isthmus? Were they aboriginals— some type of humanity which, blended with all sorts of races, has melted away and left no human trace except some occasional and abnormal form, such as Nature throws out from time to time like recurrent thought in the cosmic mind, some dim recollection of a vanished past? Who were they? They themselves believed that they were autochthones of the soil. In their legends they tell how their first ancestors rose from the black mud of the Nile before the Creator finished the world, so anxious were the gods to behold their birth, and they gave their country the name of "Chemi," meaning "the land of the black people."

The greatest authority upon Egypt alive today and the man who has done more actual excavation work in Egypt than any other, living or dead, William Flinders Petrie, asks in his great work upon Egyptian history: "Whence came the invading race— the high caste race— who founded the dynastic history? The ancient writers considered them Ethiopians and that they came from the south, and certainly in no other quarter, Libyan, Syrian or Anatolian, can we find an analogous people." Again, from his lecture upon "Religion and Conscience in Ancient Egypt," he says, in reference to a statue discovered in Egypt: "There is a coarse type of mulatto appearance; and as it is certain anatomically that there is much Negro blood in the oldest Egyptians, we have one element of the mulatto in evidence."

Juba, the Numidian king and writer, says: "The Ethiopians assert that Egypt is one of their colonies; there are striking likenesses between the laws and customs of both lands; the kings wear the same dress and the uraeus adorns their diadem." There is much more to substantiate this close relationship. In consulting the Egyptian inscriptions we find that without exception the south always comes first. The kings of the south are always mentioned before the kings of the north. In the mythological inscriptions we read that Horus first resided in the south, and, coming down the river, conquered the country as far as the sea. The Egyptian ever looks in the direction from whence his god came.

To sum up the results obtained and the conclusions to be drawn from the study of the Egyptian monuments and remains, no better quotation can be used than one from an address of Dr. Rudolph Virchow, the famous founder of that branch of medicine known as cellular pathology. This eminent scientist was requested by the great German Anthropological Association to go to Egypt and study the monuments, temples, statues and other remains of the Egyptian civilization, and bring back some authoritative decision as to the racial relations of the Egyptian people. He remained in Egypt two years and on August 5, 1889, he delivered his answer to the association. His address began as follows: "I thought I could find by comparative examination of the living and the remains and pictures of the dead some points establishing the change of the ancient Egyptians into the Egyptians of historic times, but I have returned with the conviction that ancient Egypt and its neighboring countries have not essentially changed during all these periods. If Menes really existed, then the Egyptians in his times were Negroes, since quite old mural paintings show Negroes with all their peculiarities." Almost identical is the conclusion reached by Edouard Naville, the famous French archeologist, who startled the world a few years ago by discovering the tomb of Osiris, now one of the most wonderful ruins in Egypt. In his lecture upon "The Origin of Egyptian Civilization," delivered before the Royal Anthropological Institute, he compares all the great theories as to the racial origin of the Egyptians and then, after reviewing his own facts, gathered after years of research, says: "It (Egypt) belongs to a nation formed by an indigeneous stock, of African origin, among which, settled conquerors coming from Arabia, from the same starting point as the Chaldeans. This explains a certain similarity between Egypt and Babylon. The foreign element was not Semitic. They belonged, like the natives, to the Hamitic stock; therefore they easily amalgamated with the aborigines, into whom they infused their more progressive and active spirit. The dawn of the Egyptian civilization is certainly a distinct proof of the important part played by Africa in the history of human culture."

The religous ideas of a people often furnish us with more or less conclusive evidence as to thier racial relations, and many writers today, who get no nearer to Egypt than the armchairs in their libraries, often try to prove that because certain things in the Egyptian system of religion resembled the systems of other nations that, therefore, the Egyptians must have been something other than   African. Yet even here they miss or deliberately overlook the greatest fact of all. The old idea of man having been created in the image of his Maker is made manifest in all systems of religious worship, and the gods are ever representative of their worshippers. Therefore when M. Maspero informs us in his inestimable work upon the Egyptian religion that Osiris, the supreme god of Egypt, was "beautiful of face, but with a dull, black complexion," it is by no means improbable to conclude that his color is an index to the color of his worshippers. If, then, the black skin was in any way despicable to the old Egyptians; if men of that color were known to them only as servants and slaves; if they themselves were white-skinned Libyans or yellow-skinned Semites, it will be difficult to persuade a fair-minded people that the Egyptians would so far depart from the ideals and traditions of their race as to give Negro features and a black skin to the personification of the highest conception of the human mind---that infinite and unfathomable power that rules omnipotent to all men and gods, whose empire encompasses the earth and seas, the eternal stars and everlasting suns, and stretches to the uttermost confines of this mighty universe!

There may be many who, in spite of all that has been written, are not willing to accept what has gone before as conclusive. Men are fallible and religions questionable, and the statements of either or both may not prove absolute. But there are proofs greater than these, proofs wrought in wood and stone that have defied the wear and tear of time. From the wooden panels of the mythic period of Menes to the stone statues of the last dynasties eternal testimony is borne to the race whose labor brought them forth. Whether upon wood, limestone or granite, in the colossi cut in the flanks of the mighty sandstone hills, or in the minute images of its gods and kings carved in the stones of signet rings, the Negro features are forever apparent. Had this black been but a slave, why should his features be immortalized in enduring monuments by a nation in everlasting testimony to their unbounded pride and immeasurable glory?

And shall men ever tire of wondering at those monoliths that stand so silently beside the Nile? Will patience ever again rear pillars so vast as Karnac's, or love carve out such monstrous tombs in the quiet of rocky hills? "Time mocks the world," says an Arab proverb, "but the Pyramids mock time." With that persistency that comes from pride they cut a thousand wónders from the granite of the upper Nile and from their love of repose that lay in monumental calm they embodied their highest conception in that lonely figure which stands today the greatest and grandest monument ever chiseled by the hand of man. Those who have gazed upon that silent face will forgive the vanity of the Little Corporal, who said, as he marshalled the armies of France beneath its gaze, "Forty centuries look down upon you!" They will forgive, too, the vanity of the powerful Masonic fraternity that chose it as the symbol of their highest degree. It is the Sphinx, of which Ebers said, "At the present day it has acquired a hideous Negro aspect chiefly from the loss of the nose." He might have gone further to explain that the Sphinx has always worn that Negro aspect and that it is the face of Horus, son of Osiris, the great black god ot ancient Egypt. But Ebers is the first I have ever known who calls the expression of that calm, quiet, serene face "hideous." It may be that the sense of vision is misused by those who see in that Negro profile the contradiction of all their ethnic philosophy, but let it pass. Despite its appearance to so eminent a scholar, it nevertheless reigns today the very incarnation of African genuis.

Our own Mark Twain has paid the Sphinx this beautiful tribute: "After years of waiting it was before me at last. The great face was so sad, so earnest, so longing, so patient. There was a dignity not of earth in its mien and in its face a benignity such as never anything human wore. It was stone, but seemed sentient. If ever image of stone thought, it was thinking. It looked toward the verge of the landscape, yet looking at nothing—nothing but distance and vacancy. It was looking over and beyond everything of the present and far into the past. It was gazing out over the ocean of time—over lines of century waves, which, further and further receding, closed nearer and nearer together, and blended at last into one unbroken tide, away toward the horizon of antiquity. It was thinking of the wars of departed ages; of the empires it had seen created and destroyed; of the nations whose birth it had witnessed, whose annihilation it had noted; of the joy and sorrow, the life and death, the grandeur and decay, of five thousand slow-revolving years. It was memory, restrospection, wrought into visible and tangible form. All who know what pathos there is in memories of the days that have departed, and the faces that have vanished—albeit only a trifling score of years gone by—will have some appreciation of the pathos that dwells in these grave eyes that look so steadfastly back upon the things they knew. Before History was born, before Tradition had being, things that were and forms that moved in a vague era which even Poetry and Romance scarce knew of, passed one by one away, leaving the stony dreamer solitary in the midst of a strange, new age, and uncomprehended scenes. The Sphinx is grand in its loneliness; it is imposing in its magnitude; it is impressive in the mystery that hangs over its story. And there is in the overshadowing majesty of this eternal figure of stone, with its accusing memory of the deeds of all ages, which reveals to one something of which he shall feel when he stands at last in the awful presence of God."

As flowers grow on a grave, so myths have sprung up around those solemn tombs. Osiris, the great, good god of Egypt, was slain by Typhon, a red-haired, white-faced, blue-eyed murderer. Typhon attempted to possess himself of the throne and Isis, widow of the dead king; but Horus, the son of Osiris and Isis, opposed him and drove him from Egypt. And because the people were fearful that their enemy might return Horus transformed himself into the Sphinx and kept watch for the coming of Typhon. And who shall say the vigil has not been kept? For thousands of years Egypt dwelt happily in the Valley of the Nile, till her warriors crossed the emerald mountains with sword in hand, inviting luxury, decay and death, and though these inevitable human consequences came, as they must always come, Horus, has never ceased his vigil. The stars which garnitured the heavens of Menes still look calmy down; the ghostly moon swims just above the palms; the sun which they worshipped and glorified shines on in unmindful splendor. And what if unbidden guests tread on holy ground? What if the lion makes the tomb his midnight haunt? Egypt has lived and played her part in the human wonder drama. But I believe that the memory we have of her may hold one lesson among the many, and that is there have been and are great potentialities in that race which gave Egypt to the sum of human things. Perhaps that Hebrew sage was truly inspired when he told how in the days to come the children of Ethiopia and Egypt should again stretch forth their hands and bring back to their immortal race the glory which lies sleeping and forgotten.

ASIA

It is still current opinion among those not in touch with the latest results of scientific exploration that Asia is pre-eminently the home of the yellow races. These races are grouped under the term "Semite" because it was accepted that they were descendents of Shem, one of the variegated sons of Noah. But today the term means absolutely nothing. So many strange and perplexing problems have arisen that there is only a distant hope of ever setting matters to rights. One thing which has been discovered, and which is creating so much suprise, is that it appears that the entire continent of Asia was originally the home of many black races and that these races were the pioneers in establishing the wonderful civilizations that have flourished throughout this vast continent. At different times invaders have come from the north and tried to conquer many of these peoples, but in most cases they found them too strong and compromised by settling among them. This amalgamation has had a tendency to lighten the color of these Asiatic races, but in no instance has the complete obliteration of the African characteristics been effected. In his masterful work on "The History of Mankind" Frederick Ratzel speaks of this problem that has caused so much worry to students who wish to give the African as little credit as possible. He says: "What further contributes to make the Negro physiognomy less strange, and brings it nearer to our wont

conceptions, is that in many of its manifestations an approach to the
Semitic type unmistakably emerges, such as one may often call Jewish in
character. There is some foundation for the view that in the Semitic type
of Jew, Arab, the Syrian, and so on, there is also an underlying mulatto
type. The resemblence of the Jews may frequently have been exaggerated,
especially among the Kaffirs, but none the less there is a germ of truth in
it."

In the great Mesopotamian valley, where flourished Chaldea, Babylon
and Assyria, evidences of the rule of African peoples have become so persistent that the most famous scholars simply attribute the glory of these
mighty empires to African blood and let it go at that. True, that the ancient writers knew these were black empires and said so, but modern man
has always had the habit of believing that the ancients never knew what
they were talking about. Perhaps Rawlinson, the renowned English traveler
and explorer, has made the admission of African influence plainer than
any other modern author. He says: "The Chaldean monarchy is rather
curious from its antiquity than illustrious from its great names or admirable because of the extent of its dominions. Less ancient than the Egyptians, it claims the advantage of priority over every empire or kingdom
which has grown up upon the soil of Asia. The Aryan, Turanian, and even
the Semitic tribes, appear to have been in the nomadic condition when
the Cushite settlers (black races) of lower Babylonia betook themselves to
agriculture,erected temples, built cities and established a strong and settled
government. The leaven which was to spread through Asiatic peoples was
first deposited on the shores of the Persian Gulf at the mouth of 'the Great
River,' and hence civilization, science, letters, art, extended themselves
northward and eastward and westward. Assyria, Media, Semitic Babylonia,
Persia, as they derived from Chaldea the character of their writing, so were
they indebted to the same country for their general notions of government
and administration, for their architecture, for their decorative art and still
more for their science and literature. Chaldea stands forth as the great
parent and original inventress of Asiatic civilization, without any rival that
can reasonably dispute her claim." Could a tribute to the black mother of
Asiatic civilization be greater?

Among scientists there are some groups who try to determine the relation of races through language and there are others who try to trace relationship through religion. Those who have studied languages as an aid are
hopelessly lost in a maze of contradictions and have practically abandoned
the hope of ever deciding anything by the means of language. Those who

have used religion as a test have fared a little better, but they today are coming to the point that the black races were really the founders of all religion. In fact, the great similarity of the religion of western Asia has been one of the chief factors in bringing about the recognition of the wonderful part played by Africans in the rise of Asiatic civilizations. One author sums up the results of this study in the following words: "From the many chants from the services of Nippur, which are known to have been borrowed from the Semites, not one has been changed by Semitic school men, so far as the words are concerned. And not only did the Sumerian (black race) create these chants and fix the forms of the services, but they *ORIGINATED EVERY GREAT THEOLOGICAL DOC-TRINE* which the Semites themselves confessed. In the matter of public services Babylonian religion cannot be regarded as Semitic in any sense. I have no doubt but that in the excavations in Semitic centers such as Nippur, Ashur, Arbela and Ninevah, may yield many more texts of this kind, but they, like those we already know, are sure to be composed in sacred Sumerian. In a measure this is unfortunate, for it is gradually removing Assyria from the discipline of Semitic studies. Only let us recognize the Babylonian religion in all its essential literary forms and doctrines is decidedly anti-Semitic, and we shall avoid much misunderstanding among ourselves."

Before leaving this region and taking up the study of Persia, let me remark that Babylon and Assyria have been among the greatest empires of the world. Their splendor and magnificence have become the by-words of men. History tells us that their cities and majestic palaces were restrospects of paradise and fairer than the uplands of dreams. Today Asia is filled with the ruins of vast temples and walls which are the wonder of every traveler who beholds them. If you should ever go to visit them, recollect the indirect tribute that Ferguson, author of that monumental work upon "The History of Architecture," pays the African when he says: "No Semite and no Aryan ever built a tomb that could last a century or was worthy to remain so long."

If you have ever studied the history of Persia you will remember that historians classify it as the first great white civilization in the history of the world. So wonderful was the Persian empire, and so magnificent was its civilization, that one cannot well blame the historian for trying to claim it for the white race to the exclusion of all others. But the claim has fallen before the modern study of the Persian people. The primitive civilization of Persia has been called Elamite, and the Elamite, let it be said, was a branch of the great African federation of races. J. de Morgan in his work on Persia tells us: "Besides the Sumerian civilization in Babylonia we have in the valley of the Farum, in Persia, evidence of an early civilization which we call Elamite, which is only being explored. Whether the Elamites and Sumerians were akin, and how early Elamite civilization was, we do not yet fully know; but certainly the cunieform script was in use there also at a very early period." I quote this to impress upon you the fact that the cunieform script, so often spoken of by students and writers of ancient civilizations, was that form of writing primitively and exclusively used by that great confederation of African peoples who inhabited Asia.

We discover in Grecian mythology that Perses was the founder of the Persian race. Now, Perses was the son of Perseus, the famous hero who sprang from the Argive race, an African people who settled in Greece, and Andromeda, a princess of Ethiopia, whom Perseus rescued from death imposed upon her because her mother boasted that her daughter's beauty surpassed that of the Neriads. Couple this with the significant fact that in "The Shah Nameh," the persian epic, we find that the first ruler of Persia, Kaimers, was an Ethiopian, and that he clad himself and his people in tiger skins, because the tiger skin was the symbol of royalty among the Ethiopians, and you will begin to see how important myths and traditions are in establishing the relationship of races and nations. In this same epic we read that Zohak, one of the great Persian heroes, was none other than Nimrod, the mighty African hunter and builder, mentioned in the Bible. We read also of many princes of Persia who married Ethiopian and Yemenitic women, and it would not be out of place here to mention that later in her history, when Persia was besieged by enemies, her king sent an embassy to Ethiopia, carrying her precious epic and the Persian crown jewels, and asking the Ethiopians if they would keep them safe until Persia was free from her enemies. Ethiopia kept them for eighty years and returned them all safely when Persia asked for them again. When the Persian king received them from the Ethiopians he said in his speech of thanks that Persia never feared for their safety because "of the kinship that exi. ̄be-tween our peoples."

Berossus tells us of a Median dynasty ruling in the remotest times which was African, and even to this day wooly-haired Negro clans exist in Laristan and Mekran and even on the Helmund. The statement that the Persians were a white race is purely an invention upon the part of historians, because there is not and has never been one iota of evidence to support such a claim. There is a tradition that white Aryans invaded Persia, but if

THE CHILDREN OF THE SUN 15

they did they melted away and left no trace. In his lecture, "The Early Inhabitants of Western Asia," Felix V. Luschan says: "The old type seems to
be preserved in the Parsi, the descendants of Persians who emigrated to
India after the battle of Nahauband, of much purer form that among true
Persians. They are all short-headed and dark. I never saw Persians with
light hair and blue eyes."

The white man has always wondered from whence came and what kind
of home was originally his. About forty years ago a Professor Max Muller
decided to find out. He was a student of languages and discovered that
three root words in English were similar to three root words in Sanskrit.
Upon such flimsy evidence he propounded what is known as the Aryan
theory. He declared-that the white race came from India and how, "when
the first ancestors of the Indians, the Persians, the Greeks, the Romans,
the Slavs, the Celts and the Germans, were living within the same enclo-
sure, nay, under the same roof." The theory spread like wildfire and where
Muller had found only three words, other students came forth claiming
that they had found from ten to one hundred. For a time it seemed that
the white man's origin was finally settled. Everything went lovely for a
while, but later on a few French and German scholars began to get tired of
the noise made over the new theory. These were unable to figure out how
a small Aryan clan in the mountains of central Asia could send out great
colonies that marched four thousand miles to the shores of Europe. After
a bit of actual archeological work they discovered traces of primitive Europeans who were not Aryan and who did not speak the Aryan tongue and
still other non-Aryans who did. One scientist became so disgusted with the
ridiculous claims that he called it an invention of arm chair savants and
this peeved the theorists, who started again upon a hunt for the home of
the white races. Up to the present time they are still hunting. In India,
where they thought the question had been answered, they found millions
of black folk tucked away in the hills, living the lives of their ancestors and
unmindful of the wordy wars being fought over them.

When we inquire into the ethnology of the Hindus we find many facts,
legends and circumstances, which go to prove that they were primarily an
African people. When the Aryas, whoever they were, invaded India, they
gathered all the inhabitants under the term "Daysu," whom they described
as a blue-black race. An author, speaking of the Daysu, declares that everything from "their color and fat noses to their barbarous customs, manifested their relationship to the Negro races." As to their barbarous customs, it is to be expected that a white author would attempt to leave the

impression that they were no more than savages, but from the Vedic
hymns and Sanskrit epics themselves we understand that they most certainly were not. From the Ramayana and Mahabarrata, the Indian epics,
we read that these Daysu were civilized and wealthy and that they possessed wonderful cities. In one instance we read that "seven castles and nine-
ty forts," guarded one portion of their country. In the latter Sanskrit literature the invaders made alliances with the aboriginal princes, after they
found they could not conquer them, and when history at last dawns upon
the scene, we find some of the most powerful kingdoms of India ruled by
dynasties of African descent. In the epic which narrates the advance of the
invaders into southern India, one of the chieftans describes his race as of
fearful swiftness, unyielding in battle and in color like the dark blue
clouds. This blue-blackness appears in ancient pictures which illustrate the
epic. The fact that Krishna, their name for the sun god, means "the black-
ener" may have some significance.

To see the Hindu one is not likely to call him a white man. When he ven-
tured into the northwest some years ago his reputed fair-skinned cousin
could by no system of mental analysis accept him as such, and Kipling,
in the jargon of the British soldier, called him "nigger." In "The Annals of
Rural Bengal," Mr. Hunter in describing the Santali or hill tribes of India,
says that hundreds of imperceptible gradations may be traced "from the
black squat tribes of the mountains to the tall olive colored Brahmin, with
his intellectual brow, calm eyes and high but narrow forehead." Darwin
adds that in courts of justice it is necessary to ask witnesses whether they
are Santalis or Hindoos, so much are they alike. So it seems that after all
the Hindu must come under the classification of African. Huxley, in his
study of British Ethnology, states the truth when he says that, "the dark
stock predominates in Southern and Western France, in Spain, along the
Ligurian shore, and in Western and Southern Italy; in Greece, Asia, Syria,
and North Africa; in Arabia, Persia, Affghanistan and Hindostan, shading
gradually, through all stages of darkening, into the type of the modern
Egyptian, or of the wild Hill-man of the Dekan. *NOR IS THERE ANY
RECORD OF THE EXISTENCE OF A DIFFERENT POPULATION IN
ALL THESE COUNTRIES."*

If you have ever read the Bible you have read of a people known as the
Hittites. From the scriptures we do not glean that they were of any vast
account, in fact, no nation is of much account to the Jews save Israel. But
the Hittites were a great race and scientists are becoming more and more
convinced that no new history of civilization can hope to be complete

without a study of these people. Dr. Leopold Messerschmidt, the archeologist, who has done most in uncovering the ruins of the Hittites, tells us that they were "neither Aryans or Semites, but related to the great Hamitic federation of peoples who spread over the ancient world." A somewhat longer quotation from Recent Researches in Bible Lands, by Herman V. Helprecht, will give you some idea of the growing importance of the Hittites as an ancient world power. "The question, who were the Hittites? is one of interest to the student of the Bible, but equally so, or more so, to the student of history and civilization, since we now know that they were one of the important factors in the production of that civilization in which we have part. I say that in this civilization they have some part with us; for it is a fact that, with all the mighty originality of the Greek race, from which all true civilization has descended which the world has since seen, this civilization yet had its root in the imperfect civilizations—Egyptian, Babylonian, Phonecian, Hittite—that preceded it. Out from the river Nile there go a thousand channels which carry fertility to all Egypt, and this distribution of its water is the practical value of the Nile with which the agriculture is concerned; yet it is no foolish curosity that makes us ask whatfar distant lakes and branches contribute to produce that Nile. So the historian of civilization will not be satisfied to study Greece itself, and follow the course of its national development from Solon to Pericles and the Parthenon, and thence follow the dividing stream of its influence all over the modern world; but he will ask what went before its recorded history, what combination of forces it was that gave impulse to the Hellenic people, what were the crude juices out of which the Greek ferment made wine. Inasmuch as we inherit our civilization from Greece, when we ask what was the history, and what the art, of the Egyptians, the Babylonians, or the Hittites, we are asking of our own genealogical descent, and trying to trace our own intellectual ancestry back, not simply to the Greeks, but to those less gifted peoples whose imperfect civilization was the necessary condition of Greek development and accomplishment. In our search for our conclusions as to the race, language, history, and art of the Hitties, we have to go to five sources—the Hebrew Scripture, the Egyptian monuments, the Assyrian monuments, the Vannic monuments and the monuments of the Hittites themselves. Their ancestor, Heth, was the son of Canaan who was the son of Ham. This makes them belong to the genealogical stock of the Cushites.

It would not do to neglect the Phonecians. It is fortunate for civilization that the chosen people failed to rid the coast of Syria of the race of

Canaanites who held it, because this race became the most dauntless colonists and mariners of the ancient world. They were the first who turned their frail ships to the mercy of unknown seas, and, under the Greek name of Phonecians, explored the known world. In the words of Bosworth Smith, "It was they, who, at a period antecedent to all contemporary historical records, introduced written characters, the foundation of all high intellectual development, into that country which was destined to carry intellectual culture to the highest point which humanity has yet reached. It was they who learned to steer their ships by the sure help of the Polar Star, while the Greeks still depended upon the Great Bear; it was they who rounded the Cape of Storms, and earned the best right to call it the Cape of Good Hope 2,000 years before Vasca de Gama. Their ships returned to their native shores bringing with them sandal wood from Malabar, spices from Arabia, fine linen from Egypt, ostrich plumes from Sahara. Cyprus gave them its copper, Elba its iron, the coast of the Black sea its manufactured steel. Silver they brought from Spain, gold from the Niger, tin from the Scilly Isles and amber from the Baltic." And who are they? Historians might have accepted the legend that their country was settled by Canaanites, descendants of Ham, and let it go at that; but they were not satisfied to do so. In their desperate effort to take every shred of glory from the African race, they claimed that they were Semites. The results of archeology turn their pitiful efforts into something of a joke. Many sarcophagi have been recovered and all reveal the same African features. An official description of the sarcophagus of Esmunazar II., King of Sidon, and one of Phoencia's great historical rulers, reads "The features are Egyptian, with large full almond shaped eyes, the nose flattened and the lips remarkably thick and somewhat after the Negro mold. The whole countenance is smiling, agreeable and expressive beyond anything I have ever seen in the disinterred monuments, of Egypt or Ninevah." I leave it to you, gentle reader, if Aryan or Semite ever looked like that.

Phonecia's greatest colony was Carthage. "No native orator whose writings have come down to us, has sung of the origin of Carthage, or of her romantic voyages; no native orator has described, in glowing periods we can still read, the splendor of her buildings and the opulence of her native princes; no native annalists have preserved the story of her long rivalry with the Greeks and Etruscans, and no African philosopher has moralized upon the stability of her institutions or the cause of her fall." (Bosworth Smith.) And yet, what one of us but has heard the name of Carthage? The love of Dido is classic forever; Hanno's name is secure as one of the world's earliest and greatest navigators; and Hannibal, we cannot think of Carthage unless we think of him. Search all the pages of human history and choose a conqueror who is worthy of a place beside this black general! A man who can create armies out of merceneries, marches them thousands of miles to the foot of the Alps, nor pauses when he faces their forbidding dangers. In spite of the bitter cold, the chilling winds and the irresistible sweep of avalanches, his one cry was, "Beyond the Alps lay Italy!" Whether it was lust for gain, the love of adventure or devotion to that magnetic African, the mercenary hordes of Africans, Libyans, Spaniards and Gauls suffered a thousand deaths and rallied on to a thousand more when they heard his great voice ring down the silent chasms, "Beyond the Alps lay Italy!" The reward which comes to unalterable purpose came at last to these struggling soldiers of Hannibal and finally they stood upon the brink and gazed down into the valley of the Po. For fifteen years they and their leaders wandered at will, destroying army after army sent against them, and what if they did fail at last—did they not accomplish a feat unexampled by any army of the world? He was truly of the lion's brood.

At the time when the United States was presented with a statue of Frederick the Great, the well known journalist, Ambrose Bierce, wrote with his accustomed sarcasm and stinging truth, "The others are to be Alexander the Great, Caesar and Napoleon. Hannibal, a greater soldier than any of them, is excluded—probably because of his African descent, though he may occupy a Jim Crow pedestal later." The only fear I have is that when the truth of history is known, the United States will Jim Crow the whole of ancient history, because it is nothing but a record of African achievement and glory.

It is a paradox that the most mixed people of the world should claim itself a pure race and refrain from the miscegenation which was so universally practiced by its ancestors. I refer to the Jewish race. Of them Cheyne, the famous Biblical scholar, says: "It was as little a nation of pure blood as any on earth, for it admitted persons of Aramean and Egyptian descent as well as the Canaanitic, Hebrew and Arabic elements." To begin with, the Hebrew race and language are not paternally of Semitic origin. The original home of the people appears to have been in regions round about Arabia, regions which have always been the strongholds of African races. The Hebrews, themselves, claim that Abraham was their universal ancestor and came from Ur of the Chaldees, and this legend brings to our minds two things, firstly, that Chaldea was purely Cushite and, secondly, that Abraham is also claimed an ancestor by a great many African tribes. The legend that Israel was in bondage under Egypt for five hundred years would presuppose that considerable mixture took place, but surely if it had not done so, it did so after the Israelites came to their promised land, Canaan. Here was another nation almost purely African and among them the Hebrews made their home. On more than one occasion their chief god, Jahve, reprimanded them for associating too intimately with the black trash of the neighborhood. Solomon, whom records say was black, goes so far as to forsake the gods of Israel for the gods of Canaan and even built temples to them. Moses and many other of the leading characters had black wives and what the greatest men did is but an index to what the others might have done. In the third century, towards the close of the year 225, Dio Cassius, a Roman senator, in alluding to the Palestinian wars, says that besides the original Jews of Judea, "there are other men, who, although of a different race, have adopted the laws of the people." Further on he makes mention of the fact that a great proportion of the ancient Jews were the descendants of converted pagans, so it seems that their mixing proclivities were continued down to a very late period of their history. The tribes of black Jews which are found in Palestine, Persia, Australia, Malabar, Afghanistan, Abyssinia, Arabia, and northern Africa, are all vexing questions and, what complicates the matter still more, these black Jews insist that they are the original Jews and the others a bastard race.

"And Ishmael, the son of Abraham by his hand-maiden Hagar, went into the far country of Yemen and there took unto himself a wife, and from them descended the pure Arabian race." This is the ancestry claimed by the southern Arabians for their race and whether it be true or only a legend, they have contended for this ancestry throughout the centuries and to this day. From the north there came another people calling themselves Arabians. They were lighter in complexion than those of the south and they claimed themselves the real Arabians. The Yemenites, from whom Ishmael chose his bride, were a black race akin to the Ethiopians, and the Arabs of the south were likewise black, and between the northern and southern Arabians there broke out a hatred which they carried to the farthest ends of the world. Even after the conquest of Spain precautions had to be taken against civil war by providing that the southern Arabs settle in different district from the northern. Early in their national history two great dynasties were representative of the House of Rabia and the House of Mudar. They were the Umayyads or northern Arabians, and the

Abbasids, or southern Arabians. The Abbasids were the black Arabs and there symbol throughout their national existence was a black banner.

In early Arabian history the seat of the Umayyad dynasty was at Damascus and for a long period they ruled the whole of northern Arabia unmolested, while the Abbasid ruled the south. But suddenly the blacks arose, overthrew the Umayyad dynasty, the great Persian empire of the Sasanians, and defeated the Roman legicns of the Lower Empire. One burst of enthusiasm, it was but a flash, and these black-skinned warriors went forth to conquer the world. The result of this human convulsion was the total destruction of the northern empire and the establishment of the Abbasid caliphate. This vast empire extended from the Indus to the Atlantic and from the Caspian to the cataracts of the Nile. The capital was removed from Damascus to Bagdad, from which center radiated all that was grandest in Arabian history. For five centuries the caliphs of Bagdad reigned and their rule marked the beginning of a Moslem as opposed to an Arabian Empire.

An English authority speaking of this period, says: "It seemed as if the whole world from caliph down to the humblest citizen suddenly became students, or at least patrons of literature. In quest of knowledge men traveled over three continents and returned home, like bees laden with honey, to impart the precious stores which they had accumulated to crowds of eager disciples, and to compile with incredible industry those works of encyclopediac range and erudition from which modern science, in the widest sense of the word, has derived more than is generally supposed." It was under the rule of these dusky sovereigns that the Arabian Nights were compiled and rewritten, the Rubaiyat composed, that Hafiz flourished, and that the Romance of Antar was created.

Let me speak a moment of the Romance of Antar. I have searched in vain to find it quoted in any American book, although it is the greatest lyric poem of Arabia. Can it be because the hero describes himself as being "black and swarthy as an elephant?" Stranger still, Antar was not an Arabian born, but a Negro slave, yet is chosen among the Arabs as the fullest expression of their own ideals of a hero. Even in the cities of the Orient today the loungers in their cups never weary of following the exploits of this black son of the desert, who in his person unites the great virtues of his people, magnanimity and bravery, with the gift of poetic speech. It is the Arabic romance of chivalry and to it is due the spread of romance and chivalry throughout medieval Europe.

Note, too, fact that Mohammed was of these black Arabs. When he appealed to the Arabians he called himself and "Arab of the Arabs, of the purest blood of your land, of the family of Hashim and of the tribe of Qurysh." It was the family of Hashim that founded the House of the Abbasids, and thus are we brought face to face with the fact that the third of the world's greatest religions was founded by a man in whose veins flowed black blood. This is one reason why Mohammedanism is so strong and will ever remain strong among the races of Africa. The religion preaches absolute equality and one of the precepts of the Koran reads, "If a Negro is called to rule over you, hear him and obey him, though his head be like the dried grapes." From what has been written of the Jews and Hindus it will readily be seen that the African is now as he was in the dawn of history, the founder of religion.

The spread of Mohammedanism included the whole of north Africa and, in time, penetrated Spain. It found Spain a desert and a wilderness and turned her into a garden of beauty. Never before nor since has she seen such glory as was hers when the Moors reached Toledo, Seville and Granada, the most beautiful cities of Europe. Cordova became the educational metropolis of civilization, Seville became the literary center of the world, and Granada was the triumph of wonderful architecture. Spain was never anything until these Africans, Negroes if you will, made her a land of flowers, wine, music, art, beauty, and love. Her history is all of them— the record of their glory and their fall. She became exquisite in the warm sun of Islam and withered away when the northerners conquered her. Read Draper's Intellectual Development of Europe and you will get some idea of the vast influence which these swarthy people exerted upon the civilization of Europe. To them was due the Rennaissance.

And this ends the survey of Asia. Fifty years ago one would not have dreamed that science would defend the fact that Asia was the home of the black races as well as Africa, yet it has done just that thing. Now when we gaze on the ruins of Assyria's palaces or stand in wrapt wonder before the fallen winged beasts which guarded her gates; when we stand silently upon the spot that once was Babylon and ponder upon the mighty walls built by this grand and wondrous mistress of the Euphratean plain or reverently uncover before the tumbled pillars of sanctuaries built in the long ago to forgotten gods; when we marvel at the depth of love and the majesty of grief that built the Taj Mahal or scan the perfumed literatures of India and Persia and Arabia, let us not forget that the secret, like the secret of all things wonderfully and aesthetically beautiful, lies with Africa, the mother of civilization and of nations.

EUROPE

I imagine that when I claim that the Grecian civilization was of African origin, you will grant that it is hardly in keeping with the traditions inherited from our schooldays. There is a peculiar unanimity among all historians to state without reservation that the greatest civilization the world has ever known was pre-eminently Aryan. The old idea that it sprung, like Minerva, full armed from the brow of Zeus no longer holds good. It is true that for a while it seemed that it had no tangible beginning. The fabled kings and heroes of the Homeric Age, with their palaces and strongholds, were said to have been humanized sun-myths; their deeds but songs woven by wandering minstrels to win their meed of bread. Yet there has always been a suspicion among scholars that this view was wrong. The more we study the moral aspects of humanity the more we become convinced that the flower and fruits of civilization are evolved according to laws as immutable as those governing the manifestations of physical life. Historians have written that Greece was invaded by Aryans about 1400 B. C. and that henceforth arose the wonderful civilization, but the student knows that such was an impossibility and that some vital factor had been left out of the equation. When the Aryans invaded Greece they were savages from Neolitic Europe and could not possibly have possessed the high artistic capacities and rich culture necessary for the unfolding of Aegean civilization. "Of thorns men do not gather figs, nor of a bramble bush gather they grapes."

Speaking of the two foremost Grecian states, Herodotus writes as follows. "These are the Lacedaemonians and the Athenians, the former of Doric the latter of Ionic blood. And indeed these two nations had held from very early times the most distinguished place in Greece, the one being a Pelasgic the other a Hellenic people, and the one having never quitted its original seats, while the other had been excessively migratory."
"The Hellenes, wrote Prof. Boughton in the Arena some years ago, "were the Aryans first to be brought into contact with these sunburnt Hamites, who, let it be remembered, though classed as whites, were probably as strongly Negritic as are Afro-Americans." "Greek art is not autochthonous," said Thiersch some fifty years ago, "but was derived from the Pelasgians who, being blood relations of the Egyptians, undoubtedly brought the knowledge from Egypt." "The aptitude for art among all nations of antiquity," remarked Count de Gobineau a few years latter, "was derived from amalgamation with the balck races. The Egyptians, Assyrians,Greec-

ians, and Etruscan were nothing but half-breeds, mulattoes." In the year
1884, Alexander Winchell, the famous American geologist, upset Americans with an article appearing in the North American Review. From it I
quote the following: "The Pelasgic Empire was at its meridan as early as
2500 B.C. This people came from the islands of the Aegean, and more re-
motely from Asia minor. They were originally a branch of the sunburnt
Hamitic stock that laid the basis of civilization in Canaan and Mesopotomi-
a, destined later to be Semitized. Danaos and his daughters—that is, the
fugitive 'Shepherds' from Egypt—sought refuge among their Hamitic
kindred in the Peloponesus about 1700 B.C. Three hundred years before
this these Pelasgians had learned the art of weaving from Aryan immigrants
In time they occupied the whole of Greece and Thessaly. Before 200 B.C.
they established themselves in Italy. Thus do we get a conception of a vast
Hamitic empire existing in prehistoric times, whose several nationalities
were centered in Mesopotomia, Canaan,Egypt, Northwest Africa, Iberia,
Greece, Italy, Scily, Sardinia, and Central Europe—an intellectual ethnic
family, the first of the Adamites to emerge into historic light, but records
of its achievements buried in gloom almost as dense as that which covers
the ruder populations that the Hamites everywhere displaced. To this
family, chiefly, are to be traced the dark complexions of the nations and
tribes still dwelling around the shores of the Mediterranean."
    It was to be expected that such statements as the foregoing would
throw the whole scholastic world into a ferment. There was a scramble to
bolster up the cause of Aryanism and to preserve this greatest of all civilizations, at least, to the credit of the Caucasian race. Homer was scanned
with a patience unknown to college students and the classic myths were re-
fined in the alembics of master minds. Yet there were some who cared
more for truth than for racial glory and among them was Dr. Schlieman.
Armed with a spade he went to the classic lands and brought back to light
a real Troy; at Tiryns and Mycenae he laid to view the palaces and tombs
and treasures of Homeric kings. His message back to the scholars who wait-
ed tensely for his verdict was, "It looks to me that this civilization belonged to an African people." A new world opened to archeologists and the
Aegean became the mecca of the world. Traces of this historic civilization
began to make their appearance far beyond the limits of Greece itself.
From Cyprus and Palestine to Sicily and southern Italy, and even to the
coasts of Spain, the colonial and industrial enterprise of the "Myceneans"
has left its mark throughout the Mediterranean basin. The heretics were
vindicated.

The next great scientist to make extensive explorations in these classical regions was Dr. MacKenzie. After he had spent much time in excavating "the houses of Minos," he wrote: "It is unquestionable that the whole region of the Mediterranean was first peopled by Hamites, and the races who were the bearers of the Aegean civilization came from the south." Sir Arthur Evans, elected last year as president of the British Association, also made very extensive researches in Greece and on the Isle of Crete, and before the London Hellenic Society a short time ago, he remarked: "Whether they like it or not, classical students must consider origins. The Greecians whom we discern in the new dawn were not the pale- skinned northerners, but essentially the dark-haired, brown-complexioned race." I might further mention that Prof. Sergi of the University of Rome, has founded a new study of the origin of European civilization upon these remarkable archeological finds and titled, The Mediterranean Race. From this masterly work I choose the following quotation, "Until recent years the Greeks and Romans were regarded as Aryan, and then as Aryanised peoples; the great discoveries in the Mediterranean have overturned all these views. Today, although a few belated supporters of Aryanism still remain, it is becoming clear that the most ancient civilization of the Mediterranean is not of Aryan origin. The Aryans were savages when they invaded Europe; they destroyed in part the superior civilization of the Neolithic populations, and could not have created the Greco-Latin civilization. The primitive populations of Europe originated in Africa and the basin of the Mediterranean was the chief center of movement when the African migrations reached the center and north of Europe.

What, then, are some of these discoveries which have so completely destoyed this ethnic fetish of the Caucasian race? The greatest and most conclusive of them all was the discovery of the palace of Minos by Sir Arthur Evans. In 1894 this scientist undertook a series of exploration campaigns in central and eastern Crete. It had so happened that some years previous he had been hunting out ancient engraved stones at Athens and came upon some three or four sided seals showing on each their faces groups of hieroglyphic and linear signs distinct from Egyptian and Hittite, but evidently representing some form of script. Upon inquiry Sir Arthur learned that these seals had been found in Crete, and to Crete he went. The legends of the famous labyrinth and palace of Minos came back to him and were refreshed by the gossipy peasants who repeated the tales that had come down as ancestral memories. In wandering around the site of his proposed labors Sir Arthur noticed some ruined walls, the great gypsum blocks of

which were engraved with curious symbolic characters, crowning the southern slope of a hill known as Kephala, overlooking the ancient site of
Knossos, the city of Minos. It was the prelude to the discovery of the ruins
of a palace, the most interesting archeological find of modern times.

Who was Minos? In the myths that have come down to us he was a
sort of an Abraham, a "friend of God," and often appears as almost
identical with his native Zeus. He was the founder and ruler of the royal city of Knossos, the Cretan Moses, who every nine years repaired to
the cave of Zeus, whether on the Cretan Ida or Dicta, and received from
the god of the mountain the laws for his people. He was powerful and
great and extended his dominions far and wide over the Aegean Isles and
coast lands, and even Athens paid him tribute of men and maidens. To him
is attributed the founding of the great Minoan civilization, the civilization
which mothered that of the Greek.

It is no place here to review the mass of archeological data which
the discoverers of this civilization have produced. They consist of cy-
clopean ruins of cities, strongholds, tombs, vases, statues, votive bronzes,
and exquisitely expquisitely engraved gems and intaglios. That which is
most valuable in establishing the claim of the African origin of the Grecian
civilization is the discovery of the frescoes on the palace walls. These
opened up a new epoch in the history of painting and are of the utmost
interest to the world. The colors are almost as brilliant as when laid down
three thousand years ago. Among them are numerous representations of
the race whose civilization they represent. It was a race neither Aryan or
Semitic, but African. The portraitures follow the Egyptian precedent and
for the first time the mysterious Minoan and Mycenean people rise before
us. The tint of the flesh is of a deep reddish brown and the limbs are
finely moulded. The profile of the face is pure and almost classically
Greek. The hair is black and curling and the lips somewhat full, giving the
entire physiognomy a distinct African cast. In the women's quarters the
frescoes show them to be fairer, the difference being due, probably, to the
seclusion of harem life. Yet in their countenances, too, the features
distinguish them as of African blood.

But these frescoes of ancient times need not be such a surprise to
scholars and public after all. The very classics themselves have more than
hinted of the great part played by Africa in the development of Grecian
civilization. Let us revert to the myths and trace the descent of Minos and
his progent. You will recollect that the ancient heroes of Greece were divi-
ded into the older and younger heroes, the former belonging to the House

of Inachus, distinctly Hamitic, while the latter belonged to the House of Japetus, distinctly a mixture. The Pelasgic races of the south traced their descent from Inachus, the river god and son of Oceanus. The son of Ianchus, Phoroneus, lived in the Peloponesus and founded the town of Argus. He was succeeded by his son Pelsagus, from whom the aforementioned races of the south derived their name. Io, the divine sister of Phoroneus, had the good fortune, or perhaps misfortune, to attract the attention of the all-loving Zeus and as a consequence incurred the enmity of Hera. She is transformed into a beautiful heifer by Zeus, but a gadfly sent by Hera torments her until she is driven mad and starts upon those famous wanderings which became the subject of many of the most celebrated stories of antiquity. Aeschylus reviews her roamings in his great tragedy, Prometheus Bound, and makes Io to arrive at Mount Caucasus to which the fire bringer was bound. It is here that Prometheus delivers to her the oracle given him by his mother, Themis, Titan-born. He directs her to Canabos, a city on the Nile, and tells her that there Zeus will restore her mind:

"And Thou shalt bear a child of Zeus begotten, Epaphos,
'Touch-born,' swarthy of hue."

Aryan parents and white gods do not usually bear black children and to show that Aeschylus was thoroughly cognizant of the etnical relationship here implied, I quote from the Suppliants, another of his tragedies. The Suppliants were the fifty daughters of Danaos, the Shepherds of Egypt, and they describe themselves as, "We of swart sunburnt race," "Our race that sprang from Epaphos," and when they appear before the Argive king, claiming his country as their ancestral home, their color causes him to speak in these words:

"Nay, strangers, what ye tell is past belief
For me to hear, that ye from Argos spring;
For ye to Libyan women are most like,
And nowise to our native maidens here.
Such race might Neilos breed, and Kyprian mould,
Like yours, is stamped by skilled artificers
On women's features; and I hear that those
Of India travel upon camels borne,
Swift as the horse, yet trained as sumpter-mules,
E'en those who as the Aethiops' neighbors dwell.

And had ye borne the bow I should have guessed,
Undoubting, ye were of the Amazon tribe."

No, Aeschylus made no mistake. He meant just what he wrote and
the discoveries of the wonderful Minoan civilization have proven that the
swarthy touch-born son of Zeus and Io was the incarnation of the African
element that raised Greece to the very pinnacle of civilization. Minos is
in direct descent from Epaphos and among the latter's prolific progeny
we note such names as Agenor, Belus, Cadmus, Europa, Aegyptus, Danaus,
Perseus, Menalaus, Hercules and Agamemnon, chosen by the Greeks to
lead them against Troy. Helen, the famous enchantress, whose beauty
caused the Trojan war, was a brown-skin girl.

If I should conclude at this point, the argument for Greece would be
complete and conclusive, but let us consider the supposed testimony to
the presence of the fair type in Greece and to its superiority over the dark-
er populations—testimony adduced by certain white students who attempt
to prove that Homer affords such evidence. From the work of these indus-
trious authors one gets the idea that golden hair and blue eyes were so
common around Greece that there was little chance for any other kind to
linger. The truth of the matter is that these translators, like historians,
have permitted their prejudices to warp their accuracy. There is not in the
entire writings of Homer an adjective or description applying to any of the
principals that even suggests that a single one of them had blue eyes and
golden hair. Indeed it is quite the reverse. Athena is glaukopis; glaukos
means blue like the sea and the unclouded sky; the olive is glaukos also,
Athena is guardian of the olive. Glaukopis means that her eyes are brilliant
and terrible. Apollo in Homer is chrysaeros; that is to say, bearing a golden
sword; while xanthos, which has been mistranslated to mean fair means
brown. Artemis is eustephanos, which has no relation whatever to fair.
Neptune is kyanochaites; that is to say, bluish, blackish, like the dark deep
waves of the ocean. Neither Hera or Kalypsos are fair from their descrip-
tive adjectives. Achilles is xanthos, which as was said before means brown.
Agamemnon is also xanthos, and remember, if you please, that he is in direct descent from Epaphos, the black ancestor of the Pelasgic house.

So you see that not even the translators are to be trusted Prof. Sergi
made a special investigation of the supposed testimony to the presence of
the fair type in Greece and his conclusions are worth quoting: "In Homer
none of the individuals are fair in the ethnographic sense of the word. I
could bring forth a wealth of facts to show that what I have just stated re-

garding the anthropological characters of the Homeric gods and heroes
may also be said, and with more reason, of the types of Greek and Roman
statuary, which, in the case of the divinities they may be conventionalized,
do not in the slightest degree recall the features of a northern race."
Hence the blue-eyed, golden-haired and pale-skinned gods and godesses
that grace the canvasses of our art galleries and theater curtains are merely
camouflage— a subtle attempt to hide the truth and to perpetuate a lie.

I need not go into details concerning the ethnical relations of the Romans, since they, too, are Mediterranean and are closely related to the
same   African confederation of races as Greece. Aeneas, their mythical
founder, was in direct descent from Dardanus, the African founder of
Troy. The Aenead, like the Illiad and Odyssey and all other of the world's
great epics, is the poetic story dealing with African people.

The greatest of all Italian people to precede the Romans were the Etruscans. A great deal is not known of them, for while they have left extensive
remains, the key to the reading of their inscriptions has not yet been discovered. That they were of African-derivation is conceded, for the African
type is plainly visible in their art and statuary. "The solution of the Pelasgic problem," says Sergi, "will also be the solution of the Etruscan problem, for the relation of the Etruscan to the Pelasgians is no longer doubtful; the Lemnos inscription removes all doubt on this matter." Jean Finot,
the well known French savant and scientific scholar, says in his admirable
work entitled, "Race Prejudice"; "Not to speak of the prehistoric, and
therefore doubtful peoples, we see Italy, at the dawn of the period acces-
sible to science, two great branches of the African peoples, viz., the Libur-
ni and the Sicani." Again, Virgil informs us that the Pelasgians occupied
the Palatine, one of the seven hills of Rome. And once more choosing a
quotation from Sergi, the great Italian scholar: "The two classic civilizations, Greek and Roman, were not Aryan, but Mediterranean. The Aryans
were savages when they invaded Europe; they destroyed in part the superior civilization of the Neolithic populations and   COULD NOT HAVE
CREATED THE GRECO-LATIN CIVILIZATION.Thus it is that any one
today who studies the racial elements of Greece and Latin Italy necessarily
finds' the primitive elements of the Mediterranean prevail in greatest a-
mount, varying in different regions; the Indo-European or Aryan elements
are very rare."

And in the face of the great claims made by the white race as the devel-
opers of civilization, it is strange that wherever one takes up an intensive
study of origins the fact obtrudes itself that the Aryan elements are indeed

rare. Among the British , the French, the Swiss, the Germans and even the Irish, African elements are persistent in hair, eyes, skin and anatomical features. It is a legend among the Irish that a colony of Egyptians settled in Ireland thousands of years ago and founded the Gaelic civilization of which we have heard so much. The name Fenian is supposed to be a corruption of Phoenician, another people whom legend has connected closely with the primitive Irish.

Europe, according to scientists, was primitively occupied by three races: the Canstadt, the Iberian and the Cro-Magnon. All were African. The Canstadt and Iberian were the earlier of the two and did not show such advancement in civilization as did the Cro-Magnon. The Cro-Magnon was a nobler and more cultured race. It manifested a peculiar and striking aptitude for art. There seems to have been orders of rank among them, government and an acquaintance with agriculture and the manufacture of sun-dried pottery. They paid great respect to their dead chiefs, burying their bodies in tombs of huge flagstones placed edgewise side by side, with smaller stones laid upon the upright one to form the roof of the building . These sepulchres, the well known dolmens, have been found built on precisely the same plan in Ireland, England, the greater part of Europe, the west of Asia, Japan, India, Arabia and north Africa. The construction of these dolmens is so similar in style that we conclude that they are the work of one race. Hence arose the conclusion that in all probability the African race was the first race to spread itself over the world and to nourish the beginnings of culture which eventually showed their highest manifestations in the civilizations around the Mediterranean. Of course, as always, a few scientists have tried to prove that these races of Europe were not Africans, but the recent discovery of caves in which these races have left sculptures and paintings has ended all discussion. In the paintings the people are represented as brown and black.

And this is the story of the Children of the Sun. Not only have we been something as against the claim that we have been nothing, but we have been everything. History is all of us, the record of our rise, our glory and our civilization. We did not attain perfection; neither did others. But if worth be the measure of equality, then we claim equality with all men by reason of precedence and excellence. Until out of the mist of future years there comes a race whose ancestry eclipses ours, then and then only will we concede supremacy.

The myths tell us that Momus blamed Jupiter because in creating man he put no window in his breast through which the heart might be seen.

Momus was a sleepy god, and we mortals are likewise troubled with a lack of insight into human equations and human values. No doubt Jupiter could have done better. Man is far from a perfect creation and the superman is still a dream. But as the gods could do no more for us, may we not now do something for ourselves? Were not the eyes of Momus as much at fault as the fingers of Jupiter? If we lay aside the narrowing prejudices of birth and education, under the influence of which it is impossible to balance nicely the deeds and actions of men, may we not discover here and there openings into the human soul? May we not eventually understand that to make the earth a dwelling place of happiness is a collective task and that it can only be realized through the brotherhood of man?

A Select List of Black Classic Press Titles

The Negro
W. E. B. DuBois

Originally published in 1915, Dr. W. E. Burghardt Du Bois' "little book," as he called it, was one of the most important and seminal works on African and African American history. It was small in size but gigantic in purpose. In it Du Bois, unquestionably an eminent historian, brilliantly attempted to encapsulate the ten thousand-year record of the peoples of Africa, then referred to as "Negroes." Introduction by W. Burghardt Turner and Joyce Moore Turner.
ISBN 1-58073-032-9. 1915*, 2004. 281 pp. Paper $14.95.

David Walker's Appeal
David Walker

Walker's Appeal represents one of the earliest African-centered discourses on an oppressed people's right to freedom. African American political philosophy has evolved from many of the themes that it articulates.
ISBN 0-933121-38-5. 1929*, 1993. 108 pp. Paper $8.95.

A Tropical Dependency
Flora Shaw Lugard

When Lady Lugard sat down to write *A Tropical Dependency*, it was not her intention to inspire generations of Africans to regain the independence of their countries. Lugard writes of slavery as though it was a God-given right of Europeans to own Africans as slaves. Ironically, her text on Africa's place in history reaffirms the belief that "If Africa did it once, Africa can do it again!" Introduction by John Henrik Clarke.
ISBN 0-933121-92-X. 1906*, 1997. 508 pp. Paper $24.95.

The Name "Negro": Its Origin and Evil Use
Richard B. Moore

Moore's study focuses on the exploitive nature of the word "Negro." Connecting its origins to the African Slave Trade, he shows how the label "Negro" was used to separate African descendants and to confirm their supposed inferiority.
ISBN 0-933121-35-0. 1960*, 1992. 108 pp. Paper $10.95.

Wonderful Ethiopians of the Ancient Cushite Empire
Drusilla Dunjee Houston

Mrs. Houston describes the origin of civilization and establishes links among the ancient Black populations of Arabia, Persia, Babylonia, and India. In each case, she concludes that the ancient Blacks who inhabited these areas were all culturally related.
ISBN 0-933121-01-6. 1926*, 1985. 280 pp. Paper $14.95.

The Exiles of Florida
Joshua R. Giddings

During the early part of the nineteenth century, the United States conducted a brutal campaign to re-enslave Blacks who escaped slavery and found freedom in Native American settlements in Florida. Giddings' observations document the struggle waged by these brave Africans and their Native American hosts.
ISBN 0-933121-47-4. 1858*, 1997. 338 pp. Paper $16.95.

Ancient Egypt the Light of the World
Gerald Massey

An epic analysis of ancient origins and beliefs, this first volume of Ancient Egypt elaborates how the first humans, who emerged in Africa, created thought. In the second volume Massey examines the Precession of the Equinoxes and the old Kamite sources of Christianity.
ISBN 0-933121-31-8. 1907*, 1992. 944 pp. Paper $59.95.

A Book of the Beginnings
Gerald Massey

In volume one, Massey focuses on Egyptian origins in the British Isles. In the second volume, he explores the African/Egyptian roots of the Hebrews, the Akkado-Assyrians, and the Maori. By linking these diverse cultures and origins to their African roots, Massey demonstrates not only the extent of African influence but its durability as well.
ISBN 0-933121-93-8. 1881*, 1995. 1200 pp. Two volume set. Cloth $84.95.

The Natural Genesis
Gerald Massey

By centralizing Egypt as the root of Western civilization's myths, symbols, religions, and languages, this famed Egyptologist and 'mythographer' challenges conventions of theology as well as fundamental notions of race supremacy. Introduction by Dr. Charles S. Finch.
ISBN 1-57478-009-3. 1883*, 1998. 1087 pp. Two volume set. Paper $59.95.

Christianity, Islam and the Negro Race
Edward W. Blyden

Blyden offers an early African-centered perspective on race, religion, and the development of Africa.
ISBN 0-933121-41-5. 1887*, 1993. 441 pp. Paper $14.95.

To order, send a check or money order to:
Black Classic Press
P.O. Box 13414
Baltimore, MD 21203-3414

Include $5 for shipping and handling, and $.50 for each additional book ordered.
Credit card orders call: 1-800-476-8870

For a complete list of titles, please visit our website at www.blackclassic.com

*Indicates first year published

091222-300-12-60W